77 Awesome
CHEMISTRY
FACTS Every kid should know!

ARCTURUS

ARCTURUS

This edition published in 2023 by Arcturus Publishing Limited
26/27 Bickels Yard, 151–153 Bermondsey Street,
London SE1 3HA

Author: Anne Rooney
Illustrator: Nancy Butterworth
Consultant: Janet Bingham
Editor: Rebecca Razo
Designer: Stefan Holliland
Editorial Manager: Joe Harris

ISBN: 978-1-3988-3112-4
CH010869US
Supplier 29, Date 0823, PI 00003646

Printed in China

Welcome to the Awesome World of Chemistry!

Did you know that much of your body is more than 13 billion years old?

Or that the water you drank this morning was once ingested by a dinosaur?

Or that some metals explode in water?

Everything in the Universe is made of chemicals—and some of them are weird and wonderful. This book is packed with fascinating and awe-inspiring chemistry facts that will astound and amaze you (and some just to make you giggle).

You'll find plenty of interesting facts to ponder and discuss—and you'll be able to impress your friends and family with your science knowledge! Some of what you learn might even come in handy if, say, you fall into the Dead Sea or travel to the planet Uranus (hold your nose!).

There is no wrong way to use the book. You can start at the beginning and read straight through, or you can skip around and read whatever you find most interesting—the choice is yours. We've also included loads of illustrations. A few are matter-of-fact, but most are fun and quirky so you'll laugh while you learn.

Ready to have your socks blown off by chemistry facts? Turn the page to get started!

1 The Eiffel Tower grows in summer

The Eiffel Tower in Paris, France, is a huge metal tower 312 m (1,024 ft) tall, not including the radio antenna on the top. It's made of iron. Iron, like other metals, expands (stretches) when it's heated up and contracts (shrinks) when it gets cold. The Eiffel Tower grows a tiny bit taller on hot summer days—and shrinks a bit on cold winter days.

Lopsided

The Tower doesn't grow evenly. Only one of the four sides is in the direct path of the Sun, so it is only this side that heats up enough to "grow" longer. The result is that one side grows and the others stay the same, making the Tower lean over very slightly away from the Sun. As the Sun moves across the sky, the top of the Tower moves, too, tracing out a curve about 15 cm (6 in) across.

Heat makes things bigger

As an object heats up, the particles it's made of move more. In a solid, like the Eiffel Tower, they can't move far but they vibrate more quickly. This pushes the particles it's made of (atoms or molecules) farther apart. The object then takes up more space—its volume increases. It's called "thermal expansion." For long objects, like rods and cables, thermal expansion can be really important. No one wants a sagging cable!

DID YOU KNOW?

The Eiffel Tower was the tallest building in the world when it was finished in 1889. It was overtaken by the Empire State Building in New York, USA, in 1931.

5

2 You might be drinking dinosaur pee

The water you drink and clean your teeth with has been going round and round in the world for billions of years. It's been in all sorts of other objects and organisms. Even dinosaurs probably drank some of it—and then passed it out the other end.

Round and round

Scientists call the way water circulates through different things in the world the "water cycle." Water evaporates from the sea and the surface of the land; then it forms clouds. It later falls as rain over land and sea. Rain that falls over land can seep into the ground, run across the ground surface to be carried back to the sea by rivers, or collect in lakes. Plants take water from the ground to grow. Animals drink water from rivers, lakes, and puddles, and take in water from their food, whether it's plants or other animals. Then the water comes back out of them in their urine or breath. (You can see this if you breathe onto a mirror or window—it steams up with water from your breath.) And the water that comes out also goes back into the air, ground, or rivers to keep going around.

3 you're mostly water

Your body is made up of many different chemicals (see page 25), but a lot of it is just water. Children are about 65 percent water. Be glad you're not lettuce, which is 95 percent water!

4 Everything in the world is made of just 90 chemical elements

There are 118 known chemical elements. These are basic substances that can't be broken down into ingredients. Each element has its own design of atom that differs from the other elements. About 90 elements are easy to find occurring naturally on Earth. Some are found in only tiny amounts, and a few have to be made artifiically. All the varied substances on Earth are made from these few building blocks.

Chemicals like LEGO blocks

You could think of the atoms of the elements as being rather like different designs or shades of LEGO blocks. You can put them together in lots of combinations to make all kinds of things. When two or more atoms join together they make a molecule. A molecule can be made of atoms of the same element or of different elements. A chemical made of more than one type of atom (or more than one element) is called a "compound." The molecules of some compounds are huge and contain hundreds, or thousands, of atoms.

Your chemical body

Your body is made of atoms and molecules, just like everything else in the world. Some of the molecules are enormous. They're made of just a few elements: mostly carbon, hydrogen, nitrogen, oxygen, phosphorus, and calcium. Your body works by taking in chemicals in your food and from the air, breaking them down, and remaking them into other chemicals. You are a complex chemical factory, always making and breaking different compounds, constantly recycling chemicals.

5 Early chemists wanted to live forever

The first chemists were alchemists, who had three important goals: to turn cheap metals like lead into gold; to find the secret to eternal life; and to find the "stone of knowledge," also called the "philosopher's stone." They set their sights high!

Mix and match

Alchemists thought that the purest substance in the world was gold and that all other substances were gold with other stuff mixed in—so, gold with impurities. They reasoned that if they could get rid of the impurities, they would end up with gold. Which makes sense—or would if they had been right about it, but they weren't.

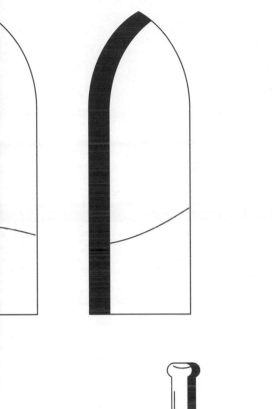

Deadly drink

The first emperor of China, Qin Shi Huang, ordered a search for the potion that would lead to eternal life. (Nobody found it!) He even drank wine laced with mercury, which he believed had led previous emperors to live for 10,000 years. Unfortunately, he died at the rather young age of 49—possibly of mercury poisoning. But he was still believed to have an eternal afterlife and was buried with 8,000 life-size clay warriors to protect him. (Which makes the afterlife sound like a dangerous place!) His tomb is said to be surrounded by rivers of mercury and booby-trapped with crossbows. No one has dared to open it yet.

Age-old chemists

Alchemy started in ancient Mesopotamia and Egypt about 5,000 years ago. That knowledge passed to the Ancient Greeks; then the Arabs; and then to medieval Europeans. Chinese alchemists had their own separate tradition—but they still hoped to find a potion that would give them eternal life.

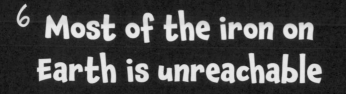

6 Most of the iron on Earth is unreachable

Iron is a common metal. In fact, there is a lot more of it than you might think—it's just that most of it is locked away in Earth's core 2,900 km (1,800 mi) below your feet.

crust

mantle

outer core

inner Core

Rocky planets are largely metal

Earth is a rocky planet. Its outer layers, the core and mantle, are made mostly of silicate rock, though much of this is hidden under a thin layer or soil, plants, worms, and cities—or water, if you're looking at the sea. Beneath the mantle, though, lies a core 3,485 km (2,165 mi) thick and 6,970 km (4,330 mi) across. And the core is made of the metals iron and nickel. That's a huge lump of metal!

Rare at the surface

There's not much iron just lying around, but there's lots bound up in rocks called ore, which people can extract by heating it to such a high temperature that the metal melts. This is called smelting. It's where we get our iron from. Even before people could make a fire hot enough to smelt iron ore, they could still get a little iron. Many meteorites (rocky lumps from space) are made of iron. Ancient Egyptians made special ceremonial objects from iron meteorites by hammering the metal into shape. The Pharaoh Tutankhamun was buried with a dagger made from meteoric iron.

Although there is lots of iron in Earth's core, we can't dig down to the core to get to it. All the iron we use comes from ore.

7 Oxygen is blue

We're used to thinking of oxygen as a gas that we can't see—that's how it exists around us, in the air. But if oxygen is cooled to -183°C (-297°F), it becomes a liquid, and the liquid is blue.

Now you see it...

How objects and substances look to us depends on how they reflect light. Sunlight includes a full spectrum, from red light to violet light. An object that reflects all the light looks white, and one that reflects none (absorbs it all) looks black. Liquid oxygen looks blue because it reflects blue light but absorbs other parts of the spectrum. To look blue, though, oxygen has to be very concentrated. A glass flask of oxygen as a gas wouldn't look any different from a flask of air.

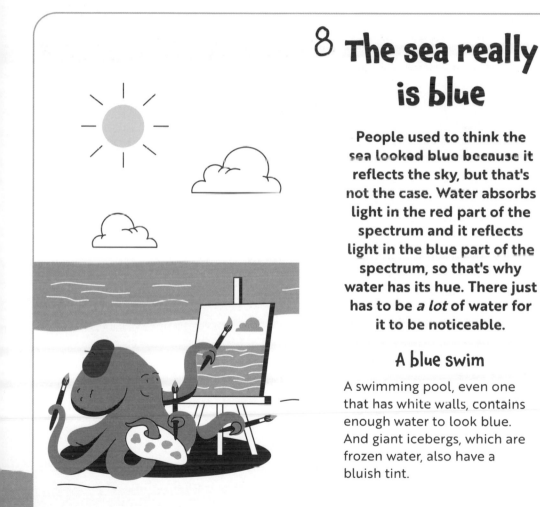

8 The sea really is blue

People used to think the sea looked blue because it reflects the sky, but that's not the case. Water absorbs light in the red part of the spectrum and it reflects light in the blue part of the spectrum, so that's why water has its hue. There just has to be *a lot* of water for it to be noticeable.

A blue swim

A swimming pool, even one that has white walls, contains enough water to look blue. And giant icebergs, which are frozen water, also have a bluish tint.

9 The worst smell in the world can make you sick

The chemical thioacetone isn't poisonous, yet it has such a terrible smell that even if you are 0.5 ki (0.3 mi) away from it, one drop can make you sick. It was discovered accidentally in 1889 by chemists in Freiburg, Germany. Their work caused vomiting, fainting, and a panic evacuation of the town.

Stinky sulfur

No one knows exactly why the stench of thioacetone is so terrible. It contains sulfur, which is probably part of the problem. Sulfurous chemicals produce the smell of bad eggs and farts.

Luckily, it's quite hard to make and keep thioacetone stable. As a red oil, it quickly changes into a smelly—but not unbearably smelly—variant at temperatures above −20°C (−4°F). However, it changes quickly, so it can't be used as a weapon.

10 Botox is one of the deadliest poisons known

Botox, or Botulinum toxin A, is used in cosmetic treatments to stop people looking wrinkly as they age. But it's a deadly poison. Just 1 g (0.03 oz) is enough to kill more than a million people.

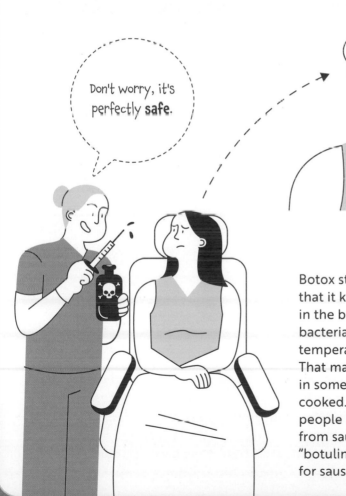

Don't worry, it's perfectly **safe**.

Wrinkles or death?

Botox stops wrinkles in the same way that it kills people: it damages nerves in the body. The poison is produced by bacteria. It is not destroyed until the temperature rises above 85°C (185°F). That makes it possible for it to remain in some food even after it's been cooked. It was discovered after many people in Germany suffered poisoning from sausages in the 1700s. The name "botulinum" comes from the Latin word for sausage.

11 Atoms "hold hands" to make molecules

Atoms group together to make molecules. A molecule can contain atoms of the same kind or of two or more different kinds. This gives us all the compounds in the Universe, from very simple compounds like water (made of just hydrogen and oxygen) to the complicated DNA that carries a recipe for a living creature and can contain millions of atoms.

Electrons as "hands"

Almost all atoms have electrons that they can give away to, or share with, other atoms to make compounds. Electrons go around the nucleus (middle) of an atom in set orbits called "shells." Atoms are stable if they have the maximum number of electrons their occupied shells can hold, and they will beg, borrow, or steal—or give away—electrons to get there.

A hydrogen atom has one electron, but it is stable with two. Two hydrogen atoms get together to share their electrons, making a hydrogen molecule. The electrons go around both nuclei.

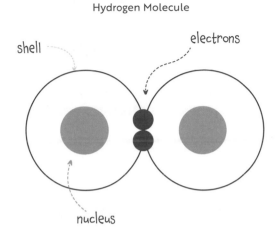

Hydrogen Molecule

shell

electrons

nucleus

A sodium atom has one extra electron and a chlorine atom needs one more, so they get together to make sodium chloride (salt), with the sodium giving away its extra electron.

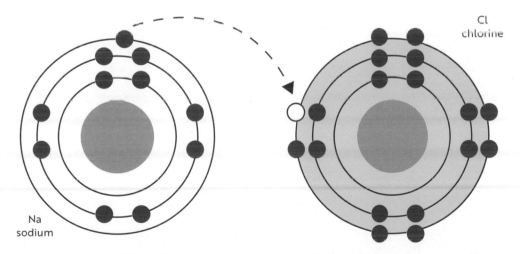

Cl
chlorine

Na
sodium

Chemists know how many electrons each atom wants to lose or gain. You can think of this as how many "hands" it has. Oxygen has two "hands," so it holds onto two hydrogen atoms, sharing an electron with each. That satisfies all the atoms and makes water.

12 you can't sink in the Dead Sea

Even a person who can't swim is fairly safe in the Dead Sea because it's impossible for a human to sink—unless they were seriously weighted down. The Dead Sea is so salty that it has a greater density than normal seawater and the human body.

Very salty!

The Dead Sea is about ten times as salty as most seawater. The whole Dead Sea contains around 37 billion tons of salt, or enough to provide cooking salt for thousands of years. If you evaporated 1,000 g (35 oz) of Dead Sea water, there would be about 250 g (9 oz) of salt left when the water had all gone.

Uplifting molecules

Water is made of molecules that have two hydrogen atoms and one oxygen atom. Salt (sodium chloride) molecules are made of one atom of sodium and one of chlorine. A sodium chloride molecule has more than three times the mass of a water molecule. These molecules make salt water heavier than plain water. The same volume of salt water has a higher mass than the same volume of freshwater, so it's denser. That means it holds you up better than freshwater. As the Dead Sea is extra salty, it's even denser and holds you up even better than most seawater. It's not good for living in, though. The salt is bad for plants and animals, and very few of them can live in the Dead Sea—which is why it's called the "Dead" Sea.

13 All the gold in the world would fit into four Olympic-sized swimming pools...

...with space to spare! The minimum size for an Olympic pool is 2,500 m³ (660,000 gal). If we melted all the gold in the world and formed it into a single block, it would have sides of 21 m (69 ft). That's all the gold that has been collected since humans began using it—there's more gold still underground.

More or less

In fact, there are wildly different estimates of how much gold has been used through history and how much is lying in places that people don't know about—hidden in ancient tombs, stored in secret bank boxes, or even just as valuables stashed away in houses. There are an estimated 52,000 tons of gold still in the ground.

14 There's gold in your phone

Gold is used in lots of modern electronics because it conducts electricity, but it doesn't corrode. It's non-reactive, meaning it won't change by forming compounds with other elements. While silver tarnishes and iron rusts, gold just stays as shiny gold forever. A typical phone probably contains about 0.03 g (0.001 oz) of gold.

Recycled

Because gold is so valuable, it's always been recycled, not thrown away. A modern gold ring might contain gold that was once worn by a Viking, a Roman, a Chinese emperor, or an ancient Egyptian princess. But now we're using gold in tiny quantities in phones, laptops, and other electronics and a lot of that isn't properly recovered later. Instead, it's just thrown away. About 10 percent of gold used now is built into electronic equipment.

15 The Milky Way tastes like raspberries

A special radio telescope in Spain is used to study the middle of our galaxy, the Milky Way, to help scientists work out which chemicals are present there. One they have found is called "ethyl formate." It's the chemical that gives raspberries their taste. If we could lick the middle of the galaxy, perhaps it would taste like raspberries!

Rum and raspberry

Ethyl formate also makes rum smell like rum. So if we could get to the middle of the galaxy—about 26,000 light years away—it would smell familiar. Chemicals produce smells by interacting with cells in the nose called "receptors." There are lots of different receptors that can be triggered by different chemicals to send a signal to the brain. The signal lets us recall a smell—such as raspberries at the middle of the galaxy!

Looking for life

Scientists are looking for chemicals vital to life using the telescope focused on the middle of the galaxy. They haven't found the chemicals they wanted to find—but they have found enough alcohol molecules in the middle of the galaxy to serve all of the grown-ups on Earth for the next 400 trillion years.

16 Metal doesn't smell if you pick it up wearing gloves

Metals don't have a smell on their own, but they can react with the oils on your hands to produce a smell.

The reaction makes a chemical that you can smell on your skin; however, wearing gloves so the metal doesn't touch your skin means your skin won't smell.

17 Sandwiches contribute (slightly!) to climate change

The lovely, squashy texture of spongy bread makes sandwiches yummy. But those bubbles in your bread are carbon dioxide. The carbon dioxide is made by the action of yeast as the dough rises. And carbon dioxide is a greenhouse gas—so it contributes to global warming.

Putting yeast to work

Yeast is a micro-organism (tiny organism), a kind of fungus. To make bread, we mix yeast, flour, and water and leave the yeast to do its work on the dough. Yeast breaks down some of the carbohydrate in flour, producing first sugars and then alcohol and carbon dioxide. Carbon dioxide produced under the surface of the dough forms bubbles. The dough is too thick and sticky for the bubbles to rise to the surface and burst, like bubbles in a fizzy drink. Instead, they are trapped by the gluey, chewy consistency of the dough. When the dough is cooked, the bubbles are captured in the bread—still full of carbon dioxide.

Don't worry!

The carbon dioxide in bread does you no harm at all. When you cut the bread, carbon dioxide in any exposed bubbles is immediately exchanged with air and any in the middle is harmless. Nor does the carbon dioxide produced by baking bread make a big contribution to climate change. It's a very, very tiny proportion of the carbon dioxide we produce. You make more by breathing than by baking bread!

18 With enough helium balloons, you could fly

If you've ever had a helium balloon, you'll know it tugs upward on its string, unlike a normal air-filled balloon. Helium balloons usually have a shiny foil envelope made of a material called Mylar.

Volume for volume

Helium atoms are smaller than all the atoms and molecules in the air around us, so helium is lighter than air. Helium balloons float because the volume they occupy is lighter than the same volume of air. To float yourself using helium balloons, you'd need enough balloons so that you and the balloons weighed less than the same volume of air. An average helium balloon can lift about 14 g (0.5 oz). So if you weigh 28 kg (62 lb), it will take $28{,}000 \div 14 = 2{,}000$ helium balloons to lift you.

Escape!

Because helium atoms are so small, they could pass through the tiny gaps in the wall of a normal latex balloon. That's why helium balloons are made of Mylar, which has smaller gaps. Mylar is also much lighter than latex, which helps it to float. But helium atoms are so small they can still fit through the gaps of Mylar and get away, though more slowly than if they were in a latex balloon. Think of pouring water through a sieve. It goes straight through. Now if you put a folded tea towel inside the sieve, the water still goes through, but more slowly.

19 Cola can make a chicken bone go bendy—it also dissolves teeth and human bones

Fizzy drinks like cola contain acids such as phosphoric acid and citric acid. Citric acid is also found in orange juice and lemonade. Given enough time, these acids will attack teeth and bones. You can test this by putting a chicken bone from a meal into a glass of cola and leaving it for a few days. It will eventually go bendy!

Concentrate!

That doesn't mean your teeth will go bendy or disappear if you drink cola. It doesn't stay in contact with them for long.

The effect an acid has depends on if it is a weak or strong acid, and on how concentrated it is. A little acid in a lot of water makes a dilute acid. Lemonade is a dilute acid. The sharp taste is produced by the acid, but it doesn't harm you. A lot of acid in very little water makes a concentrated acid. Strong, concentrated acids can be very dangerous. The acid in car batteries can eat through not just skin and bones, but even metal.

Chemists measure how strong an acid is by its pH. Liquids with a low pH are acidic and those with a high pH are alkaline, or "basic" (the opposite of an acid). Water is in the middle of the range. With a pH of 7, it's neutral—neither acidic nor alkaline—so you can drink as much as you like. A strong acid has a very low pH, and a weak acid has a pH closer to 7.

20 Mars is red because of rust

Mars has always been known as the "red planet", for its red tinge, clearly visible through a telescope. It's made of rock, just like Earth, Mercury, and Venus, but the rocks on Mars contain a lot of the metal iron. Iron reacts with oxygen to make iron oxide, or rust, which is red.

Iron outside

Mars and Earth formed from the same materials at the same time, about 4.5 billion years ago. But whereas most of the iron in Earth has sunk to the middle—resulting in the planet's iron core (see page 12)—Mars is smaller and has a weaker gravitational field; this means it didn't pull as much of its iron into the middle. It does have an iron core, but there's also a lot of iron left nearer the surface. At some point in the last few billion years this has gone rusty.

Mystery

To go rusty, iron needs to be exposed to oxygen so that it can react with it—a process called oxidation. No one knows for certain where the oxygen came from to rust Mars. It's possible that the ground went rusty when it rained billions of years ago. Or maybe sunlight broke down carbon dioxide in the Martian atmosphere, releasing oxygen to rust the planet.

DID YOU KNOW?

Mars was the god of war in Roman mythology—because the planet looks red and it reminded people of blood and bloodshed in a war.

21 Glass is made of sand

People first discovered how to make glass thousands of years ago, possibly after putting something very hot onto sand. A lot of sand is made of silicon dioxide, or silica. When it melts, it hardens into glass.

Sand everywhere

Silicon dioxide is the most common mineral on Earth—and it's everywhere. It forms quartz—a type of rock—and tiny fragments of quartz make up a lot of our planet's sandy beaches. Silica is also used by tiny, microscopic organisms called diatoms to build a hard shell around themselves. These shells are another common component of sand.

Goodbye to crystals

Silicon dioxide has a crystalline structure, which means the molecules make a regular pattern. When it's heated to 1,700°C (3,090°F), it melts. The molecules break free and swill around in no particular shape, as they do in any liquid. But as the liquid cools, they don't get back into line as they do in most other crystalline substances. They stay irregular and become glass.

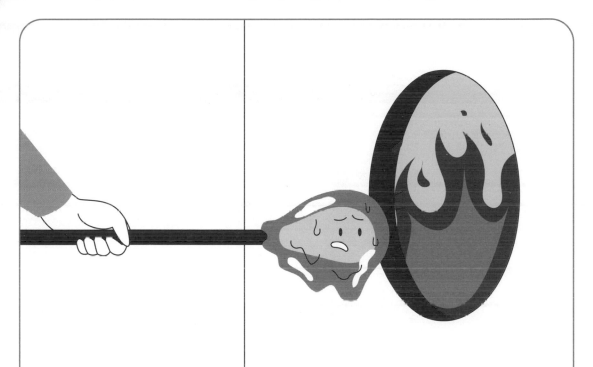

Glass isn't a proper solid

Although glass seems rock hard, it's not quite a solid in scientific terms. Chemists call it an "amorphous solid," which means a solid that doesn't hold an organized shape. Cooling molten glass slows down the movement of the molecules in it, turning it first into a super-cooled liquid. It has the disorganized molecules of a liquid, but the material is stiff like a solid. The molecules can only move a little. Cooling it even more freezes the molecules into their irregular state. They can barely move, but they aren't nice and neat like the crystals they started as.

22 Oil really does calm troubled waters

It's said that sailors used to pour their barrels of cooking oil onto a stormy sea to calm it. It gives us a phrase in common use: to pour oil on troubled waters means to calm down a situation that's getting out of hand.

It sounds crazy, but pouring oil on stormy water actually seems to work. And it might even prevent hurricanes from forming. Some scientists suggest it's because it stops droplets of water being hurled into the air by the stormy surface.

From sea to air

As wind blows over a warm tropical sea, it produces waves and lifts droplets from the surface. This creates a layer between the water and the air of mixed air-and-water. The presence of the droplets cuts friction, allowing the wind to move faster. Faster winds mean bigger waves and whips up more droplets, keeping the storm going.

Out with the oil

If sailors pour oil on to water, it spreads out over the surface forming a very thin layer. In fact, it will spread until it's only one molecule thick. The layer of oil means water droplets can't escape into the air. If the idea is correct, this slows the wind speed and so the storm can't build further.

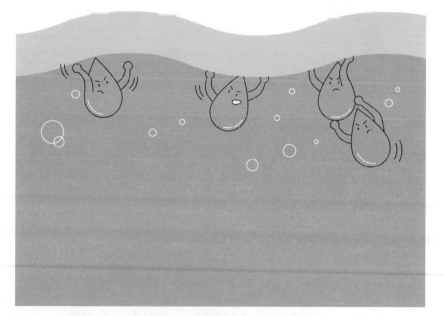

Could it be possible to prevent a hurricane happening by pouring a harmless type of oil onto the sea to stop droplets forming? Some people think it might, but it hasn't been tried yet in a proper experiment so we can't be sure.

23 There's a molecule big enough to see...

...and you see it every day! Technically, a rubber tire is just a single, giant molecule. It's made of lots of atoms, but unlike in most objects, all the atoms are chemically linked to make a single molecule.

These molecules are wheelie big!

Making bonds

Atoms of different elements often form bonds between them that hold them together in molecules. The chemical names of these substances tell us which atoms are involved and how many there are of each. For example, water has the chemical formula H_2O, which tells us two hydrogen atoms are attached (bonded) to one oxygen atom. In the organic compounds common in living things, carbon atoms are bonded to hydrogen and other atoms, often forming huge molecules with hundreds or thousands of atoms. Sometimes atoms form groups with a particular structure, called monomers, that can then link together to form even larger molecules. These are polymers; they include plastics.

Getting tough

Natural rubber is made from the sap of the rubber tree. To start with, the sap forms long, stringy molecules. In the 1830s, Charles Goodyear discovered that if he added sulfur to rubber, the sulfur molecules made bonds between the huge molecules, effectively knitting them together into a single super-molecule. That means any piece of processed rubber, however big, is really a single molecule!

Tasty polymers

Carbohydrates in the rice, pasta, bread, and potatoes you eat are made of sugars (monomers) linked together to make polymers. Because the molecules are big, they take a long time to digest. So bread keeps you full longer than sugar!

24 The world's slowest chemical experiment started in 1927...

...and it's still going. The "pitch drop" experiment was designed to show that pitch is a liquid. Pitch is a black, waxy-looking substance made from tar. It looks solid, and you can even shatter it with a hammer. But to a chemist it's a fluid because it will flow—though very, very slowly.

In it for the long haul

The pitch-drop experiment was set up by a scientist in 1927. He heated some pitch, put it into a sealed glass funnel and left it to settle for three years. Then he cut the bottom off the funnel and put a glass beaker underneath to catch the drops as they fall. And that's what it's still doing, nearly 100 years later. So far, it's formed nine drops.

Tangled mess

In a solid, molecules are held together in a fixed structure. If the solid has crystals, the structure is regular, with the molecules making the same shapes again and again, called a "lattice." Solids like plastic don't have a regular structure but have long molecules held together by bonds between them. In a fluid (liquid or gas), there are no bonds holding the molecules in place so the substance can flow freely. Pitch has long molecules, but there are no bonds between them. Instead, they're impossibly tangled. Being so tangled makes it hard for pitch to flow, but with gravity pulling the pitch to the bottom of the funnel, the molecules do very slowly work themselves free enough to move.

By the way, no one is sitting watching this experiment all the time, and sometimes the experimenters miss a drop falling.

25 Steel is more elastic than a rubber band

Steel is difficult to pull out of shape by stretching or twisting, but an elastic band is easily stretched and will distort and break. To a scientist, that means the steel is more elastic!

Being elastic

In normal life, we think of something "elastic" as something which stretches easily. In science, the definition of "elastic" is the opposite. Elasticity is the ratio of stress to strain. For a particular stretching force (stress), steel is put under less strain than rubber, because it's good at resisting the force. For that reason, it's said to be more elastic than the rubber. The more resistant to changing its shape something is, the more elastic it is.

26 The metal gallium would melt in your hand

Most metals have high melting points. They're solid at room temperature and must be heated to high temperatures to melt. But gallium melts at only 30°C (86°F), which is below body temperature.

Melting metals

In a solid metal, the atoms or molecules are arranged in a regular pattern, called a crystal lattice. As the metal is heated, the atoms gain more energy and vibrate until they can escape from the lattice. The metal becomes liquid, as it has no fixed shape. For most metals, it takes a great deal of energy to shake the atoms loose. The bonds between atoms of gallium are weaker than the bonds in many other metals, so it takes less energy—less heat—to break them and let the atoms move freely.

DID YOU KNOW?

Mercury is the only metal that is liquid at room temperature.

27 If you add salt to water, the water shrinks

Pouring a handful of salt (sodium chloride) into a cup of water makes the water level drop a little—just about two percent. That's because the molecules of water are completely random until you add the salt. Then some of them sort themselves out around the sodium and chloride ions produced by the salt dissolving. When the water is more orderly, it takes up less space.

Heavy seas

Obviously, if you dissolve salt into water, the water gets heavier because now it contains the same mass of water, plus the extra mass of salt. But the salty water takes up less space than non-salty water. This means salty water is denser than normal water. In the sea, salty water sinks to the bottom. Other factors, like different temperatures, currents, and new water flowing in from rivers, mix it all up and cause confusion. But in general, the bottom of the ocean is saltier than the water at the surface.

28 1 cup of water + 1 cup of sand = less than 2 cups of sandy water

If you mix equal volumes of sand and water, you end up with less than twice the volume.

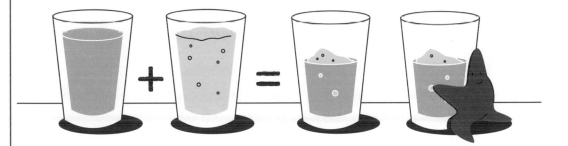

In the gaps

This is because there are tiny gaps between the particles of sand. They are usually filled with air, but the water replaces the air to trickle between them. That reduces the amount of water left over to lie on top of the sand.

29 Car airbags have an explosion inside

Does your car have an airbag? It's a bag that inflates automatically if there's a crash, making a cushion in front of the driver and front passenger to protect them. It works by making a small explosion inside a bag.

Crunch time

When a car is in a crash, it goes from moving quickly to stopping in a very short space of time. That means it decelerates (slows down) really fast. A sensor in the airbag is triggered by the deceleration to push electric current into a tiny heating element that sets fire to an explosive chemical. The heated chemical decomposes (breaks down) and produces a huge amount of gas. A gas takes up much more space than a solid, so it instantly fills the bag, turning it into a balloon. The airbag opens at more than 320 km per hour (200 mph) and fills in 40 milliseconds—that's 1/25th of a second. It's open before a person hits the dashboard or window of the car.

Gas bags

The substance in airbags is a chemical made of sodium and nitrogen called sodium azide, which is a solid, rather like salt. It's poisonous, but it's sealed inside the bag. When it's heated, the sodium azide is converted to sodium and nitrogen. Nitrogen is a harmless gas in the air. The sodium quickly combines with another chemical added just to make it safe. The airbag deflates almost immediately, the nitrogen leaking out of small holes around the bag. But as nitrogen is all around you anyway, it doesn't matter at all.

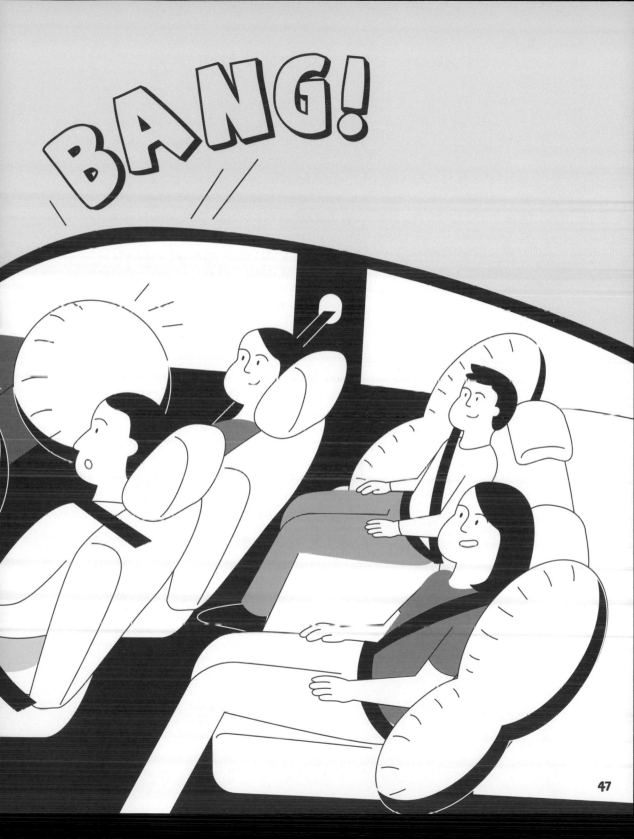

30 Uranus is a stinky planet

Uranus is a type of planet called an ice giant. It's made of chemicals that become gases above about -173°C (-279°F). The gases get denser toward the middle of the planet, even becoming liquid and slushy, but there's no distinct solid surface. Near the top of the gases is a layer of cloud, and the clouds are rich in hydrogen sulfide. That's the same chemical that gives bad eggs their very noticeable smell. The smell is so strong that if you were flying into Uranus, you couldn't miss it and would perhaps even smell it through a space helmet!

Inflammable planets

There are two gas giants: Jupiter and Saturn. They're made almost entirely of hydrogen and helium. Then there are two ice giants: Uranus and Neptune. They also contain a lot of hydrogen and helium, as well as heavier gases. One of those gases is methane, which is made of hydrogen and carbon. Another is ammonia, made of hydrogen and nitrogen, and another is water. Methane is the gas that we use to power gas cookers and boilers—it burns really well. With a supply of oxygen—which luckily they don't have—and a lighted match, Uranus and Neptune would burn!

A planet of pee and eggs?

Ammonia, one of the other chemicals in ice giants, is found in urine. In fact, it gives pee its smell. So when your spaceship had got through the layer of cloud that smells like bad eggs, you'd be heading into an area that smells of pee. It's really not a good planet to visit for a pleasant smell experience!

31 We can turn lead into gold

But it's not worth doing. Hundreds of years ago, alchemists tried all kinds of weird and wonderful techniques to turn cheap metals like lead and iron into valuable gold. It never worked. Now we can do it, by changing the atoms—but the process is so expensive that the gold produced costs more than just getting gold normally.

Blasting and smashing atoms

All atoms are made of a middle part (nucleus). Electrons orbit around the nucleus but at a great distance. (If the nucleus were the size of a basketball, its nearest electron would be orbiting at a distance of two miles away!) The nucleus contains two types of particle: protons and neutrons. What makes an atom a particular element is the number of protons in its nucleus. Hydrogen has one proton, carbon has six, gold has 79, and lead has 82. Using a huge, powerful machine called a particle accelerator, scientists can blast atoms together or smash them to bits. By smashing away three protons from a lead atom, scientists can turn the lead atom into a gold atom.

Looks like I'm going to bits!

DID YOU KNOW?

Hydrogen atoms contain no neutrons. A hydrogen atom is just a proton in the middle and one electron. It's a budget atom, cut to the bare essentials!

Heavy stuff

Particle accelerators can also make larger atoms than are ever found in nature. These break apart again quite quickly in a process called radioactive decay. Bits fall off the atom of a radioactive element, changing it from one element to another—this time to a lighter element with smaller atoms. The time it takes for half a sample of a radioactive element to change into something else is called its half-life.

Some elements disappear before your eyes

Some elements are so radioactive they decay into different elements very quickly. Livermorium, for example, has a half-life (see page 51) of 0.06 (six one-hundredths) of a second.

Cheating

Scientists can make even more unstable atoms by producing variants of elements that have different numbers of neutrons in the nucleus. These are called isotopes. Many isotopes exist naturally, but the half-life of artificial isotopes is so short they barely exist at all. Some fall apart almost as soon as they've been made. The most unstable have half-lifes of less than 0.0000000000000000000000001 second.

33 Astatine is so radioactive that it turns itself to gas

Of the elements that occur on Earth naturally, astatine is the rarest. It can't be collected into a large lump because it's so radioactive, the energy from its own radioactive decay would annihilate the lump immediately, turning it into gas.

Energy from atoms

As atoms change, they release energy. How much energy varies depending on exactly how they change and how quickly they change. The energy from radioactive decay can run power stations and explode bombs. Astatine releases so much energy as it decays that a lump of astatine would be heated up to its boiling point, so the lump would disappear into a cloud of gas—which is not very useful if you wanted a lump of astatine. Because it can't be collected to study it, chemists aren't even sure if it is a metal or not. The half-life of the longest-living isotope of astatine is eight hours. The shortest lasts less than a second.

34 you can't unbake a cake

We use chemical reactions and processes every day in our normal lives. Some of these are reversible—they can be undone—and others aren't. Baking a cake is irreversible because you can't undo the reactions that take place in the heated cake mixture.

Turn back the clock

Dissolving sugar in water is a reversible process. You can get the sugar and water back. You can boil the sugar-water, collect the steam, which condenses back to water, and the sugar will reappear as crystals. This is because neither the water nor the sugar is changed. All that happens is they become mixed up at a molecular level. It's a physical change, not a chemical one.

Changed forever

Some chemical changes can't be undone. For example, if you burn a piece of paper or bake a cake, the chemicals permanently change. Paper is made of wood pulp, which is largely long molecules of cellulose: a compound made of carbon, hydrogen, and oxygen held in a particular pattern. When you burn it, oxygen from the atmosphere combines with the carbon from the cellulose to make carbon dioxide; it also combines with the hydrogen to make water. After these chemicals change, you can't turn them back into cellulose. (A plant can, though! A plant takes carbon dioxide from the atmosphere and water from the ground and makes sugars that it later converts to cellulose.)

When you bake a cake, proteins and other large molecules in the ingredients are changed by the heat. The proteins change shape—liquid egg becomes solid, for example—and they can't be put back in their original shape.

55 Helium was first found on the Sun

There's not much helium on Earth, but there is loads in the Sun. The element was first discovered by chemists looking at the pattern of light from the Sun in 1868. They worked out that there was a new type of gas present. It was called "helium" from the Greek word "helios," meaning "sun."

Making more

Helium is produced naturally underground by the radioactive decay of other elements (see page 51). This means that more helium is constantly being produced by changing elements in the Earth's layers, rocks, and crust. Because helium atoms are small and light, they easily rise and escape into space—it's very much "here today, gone tomorrow." The exception is when people manually extract the helium from the Earth.

36 Helium crawls up a glass to escape

Like other gases, if helium is cooled to a low enough temperature, it becomes a liquid. Other liquid gases, kept cold, lie in their containers in the way we expect liquids to do. But not helium. When it's extremely cold, it crawls up the side of the beaker to get away. It becomes a "superfluid" that behaves in bizarre ways.

Up and over

Chilled to −270°C (−454°F), helium can do some odd tricks. The liquid has a viscosity of zero—it has no thickness or stickiness. The atoms start to push each other away. As they move as far apart as possible, they creep up the sides of the container and over the edge. Then they travel down the sides and drip from the bottom so that it looks as though they are leaking through the solid container!

37 Mysterious flames have lured people to their doom

Legends of "will-o-the-wisp" tell of eerie flames that appear from nowhere in boggy land. People who follow the flames have sometimes drowned in swamps, leading to legends of evil spirits luring them to their death. But the flames are entirely natural, a strange chemical phenomenon caused by burning marsh gas.

Deathly gas

As organic matter like plants and animals decays, it gives off several types of gas. One of those is methane. It's the same gas we burn in our cookers and gas fires. Two others are phosphine—gases containing phosphorus. The phosphines automatically catch fire when they come into contact with the oxygen in the air, and that bit of fire is enough to set light to the methane. The result is spooky fires that seem to wander about over bogs in the nighttime.

Burning hot and cold

We're used to thinking of fire as always being hot, but different things burn at different temperatures. Many items spontaneously combust—burn on their own, without being lit—if heated to the right temperature. Paper will burst into flames on its own at 233°C (451°F), for instance. Phosphine will burst into flames at such a low temperature that it can happen outside in a boggy marsh!

DID YOU KNOW?

A flame is just burning gas. Different flames burn at different temperatures, usually in the range 600°C (1,100°F) to more than 3,000°C (5,400°F). Blue flames are usually hotter than yellow flames.

38 Phosphorus was first found in pee

The German chemist who discovered phosphorus did so by evaporating huge vats of pee. He was doing that while trying to make a "philosopher's stone:" a legendary object alchemists sought in their quest to turn lead into gold.

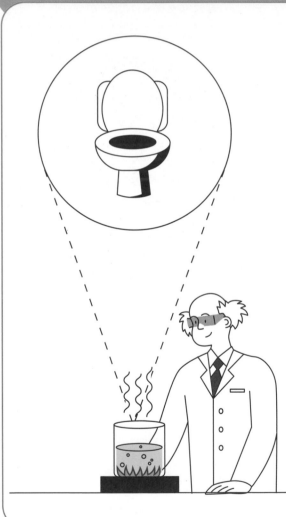

Burning issue

In 1669, Hennig Brand boiled urine until it mostly evaporated, and then heated the residue to a high temperature. It produced glowing fumes, and a liquid dripped out that burst into flames. He found if he caught and cooled the liquid, it turned into a solid that glowed. The ability to give off light like this is called "phosphorescence." Phosphorus is dangerous, though, and can spontaneously burn. Many early chemists were hurt by carrying phosphorus around.

Why pee?

Phosphorus is an important chemical in life. Our bodies use it for many things, including producing energy, making proteins and fats, regulating fluid, carrying nerve impulses, making up bones, and excreting waste.

39 Bear fossils were used to make weapons

One of the uses of phosphorus is in making bombs. During World War I, hundreds of fossilized bones from cave bears were boiled down and destroyed to provide phosphorus for bomb-making. Cave bears were a huge type of bear that lived in Europe thousands of years ago.

Bombs and bones

Bones are made of a framework of a protein called collagen, on which a mineral called calcium phosphate makes a hard structure. We need calcium and phosphorus in our diet to make healthy bones—and so did cave bears. When the bones fossilized after the animals died, the protein broke down, but the calcium phosphate remained.

40 Fireworks get their brilliance from burning metals

The salts of metals burn with bright flames of different shades. These salts are used to make the spectacular display of fireworks. The "whoosh" that sends fireworks soaring into the sky and exploding is produced by gunpowder, but the brilliant sparkles need something else.

Going up!

Lighting the touchpaper sets fire to gunpowder held inside the firework. It burns explosively, producing a lot of gas very quickly that rushes out the back of the firework, blasting it forward—which should be upward, if it's pointed in the right direction. Once the firework is up in the air, the next bit begins to burn.

Sparkling rainbows

Inside the tube, the firework is divided into sections that contain more gunpowder, a paste that holds all the chemicals together, chemicals to control the speed at which it burns, and metal salts that burn with different flames. Firework engineers can choose strontium salts to make red flames, barium salts to add green, copper salts for blue, sodium for yellow, iron for gold, and magnesium to make white.

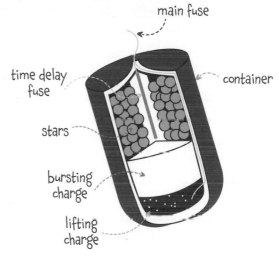

main fuse

time delay fuse

container

stars

bursting charge

lifting charge

Grounded

Not all fireworks blast into the sky. Some stand on the ground and burn from the top. The gas produced by the burning gunpowder comes out of the top, carrying the burning bits with it to create a fountain of bright light. Chemicals mixed into the firework can control the speed at which everything burns. Sparklers are hand-held fireworks, made of wire coated with gunpowder components and magnesium salts that burn slowly with a brilliant white light.

41 A dream of a snake solved a chemical mystery

Chemist August Kekulé solved a puzzle—the structure of an important molecule—with a dream; well, a *daydream*, actually. He saw in his mind a snake arranged in a circle, biting its own tail and realized the molecule was atoms arranged in a ring, just like the snake.

Puzzling poison

Benzene is a naturally occurring chemical that is used a lot in industry for making plastics and other materials. It's a poisonous liquid that floats on water (meaning it's less dense than water). Chemists long ago worked out that it's made only of carbon and hydrogen, but they couldn't work out how the atoms in the benzene molecule were arranged. The molecule has six carbon atoms and six hydrogen atoms. They knew that carbon has four "hands"—it likes to be attached to four other atoms—and hydrogen has only one "hand" (see page 18). Benzene is a stable compound, so all the atoms have made all the bonds they want and there are no hands going spare. How could it work?

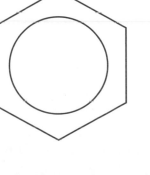

Chemists often draw the shape of benzene like this:

Seeing snakes

Kekulé pondered the problem of the structure for benzene and came up with his snake idea. He arranged the six carbon atoms in a circle, each bonded to one hydrogen atom outside the circle. That left each carbon atom with three "hands" to bond to adjacent carbon atoms. On one side, a carbon atom held out one hand, on the other side it held out two hands.

Some metals explode in water

The metals potassium and sodium react so violently with water that they burst into flames when they touch it. They're very reactive elements and are stored under oil as they would react with the air in the jar otherwise.

I'm out of here!

Bye, electron... sorry!

Electrons going spare

Sodium and potassium are both in the first column of the Periodic Table of Elements. Elements in this column have one "spare electron" in the outermost part of their atoms. The electrons in an atom all go around the nucleus, but at different distances from it. Each electron has an area its orbit occupies, called an orbital. The orbitals are arranged in groups called "shells." The shell closest to the atom has space for only two electrons. The next shell out has space for eight electrons. Electrons fill the shells from the middle out. An atom with many electrons can fill many shells, and so is larger.

Atoms are most stable when they don't have spare electrons in their outermost occupied shell. They are most reactive when they have just one electron in the outermost shell. Getting rid of the electron makes the atom stable, so they readily enter reactions that will remove the spare electron.

Whizzing in water

Potassium and sodium get rid of their spare electron when added to water because they react with the water to make a new compound (potassium or sodium hydroxide) and release hydrogen. The reaction produces heat, and hydrogen is highly flammable. The heat sets fire to the hydrogen created in the reaction, causing the explosion we see.

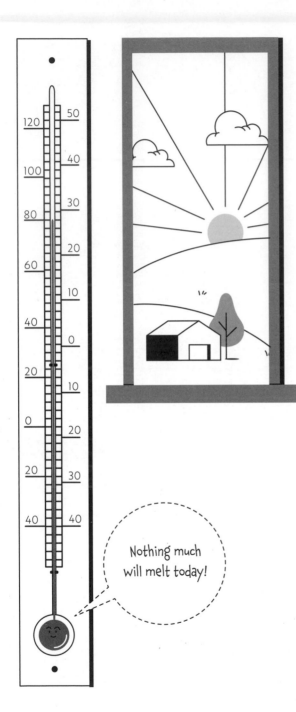

Nothing much will melt today!

43 Only two elements are liquid at room temperature

Only mercury (a metal) and bromine (a natural element) are liquid at room temperature. Whether a substance is a solid, liquid, or gas at any particular temperature depends on its melting and boiling points.

What are they like?

Most elements are solid at room temperature, but eleven are gases. The two that buck the trend have weak bonds between atoms. As a substance heats up, its atoms vibrate more. If the bonds holding the atoms into a solid structure are weak, they will soon break, allowing the atoms to move freely. This is the mark of a liquid. Bromine and mercury will become solids if cooled below their melting/freezing point.

Taking the temperature

Years ago, thermometers were made with a column of mercury in a glass tube, mounted on a scale marked in degrees of either Celsius (C) or Fahrenheit (F). As the temperature rises, the atoms of mercury jiggle about more, crashing into each other and nudging others out of the way. The more they move, the more space they take up. This means the mercury in the thermometer expands, and the column gets taller, moving up the scale—and so showing the temperature.

Tied up

Bromine is very reactive, so it's not found lying around as a brown liquid. Instead, it forms salts with other elements. Most bromine that we use is extracted from seawater. Mercury is also found locked away, usually in rocks. The metal ore is burned to release the mercury.

DID YOU KNOW?

Mercury used to be called "quicksilver," which means "living silver." It had this name because blobs of mercury slide and slither around.

44 Glow sticks make light from chemistry

When you use a glow stick, or one of those wrap-around glowing bracelets, you're harnessing a chemical reaction that produces energy in the form of light. Light from a chemical reaction is called "chemiluminescence."

Heat or light?

Chemical reactions involve making or breaking bonds between atoms. Often a reaction breaks some bonds and makes new bonds. It takes energy to break the bonds between atoms. That's why you can dissolve more salt or sugar in hot water than in cold water: the extra heat energy is used to break more bonds in the salt or sugar. Making bonds between atoms releases energy. Whether a reaction produces or uses up energy depends on the balance between the bonds broken (using energy) and bonds formed (producing energy). The energy produced is usually released as heat, but occasionally it's released as light energy. And that's what makes a glow stick glow.

dye and chemical solution

plastic casing

glass cylinder containing hydrogen peroxide

Snap!

When you bend a glow stick to start it glowing, you snap a tiny glass cylinder inside the plastic stick. The cylinder contains one of the chemicals needed for the reaction, called hydrogen peroxide. As this mixes with other chemicals in the stick, a series of chemical reactions takes place. Energy from the reactions warms up a dye in the stick, and the dye releases its energy as light—it might be yellow, green, pink, or blue depending on the dye that has been used. And so your glow stick glows!

45 There are metals you can cut with a knife

Sodium and potassium are metals, but they are very soft and very reactive (see page 66). They are so soft that you can cut chunks off a piece of one of the metals using an ordinary table knife.

Loose electrons

Sodium and potassium are soft for the same reason that they react readily with the oxygen in water and air. The spare electron at the outer edge of the atom means there are only weak bonds between the atoms in a chunk of the metal. As the atoms are only loosely bonded, it's quite easy to separate them. Scaling that up to a whole chunk of metal, it's easy to push a knife between atoms, as they're not very keen on sticking together, making the metal easy to cut.

46 Two solids make a liquid

It's possible to make an alloy (a mixed metal) from potassium and sodium, called "NaK." This has even looser bonds between the atoms—so loose that it's often a liquid at room temperature.

Runny alloy

If the mix has between 40 and 90 percent potassium it will be liquid. It's less dense than water, so it would float on water if it weren't so reactive. In fact, though, it just burns in water as both potassium and sodium do. It has to be stored in oil or a hydrocarbon liquid, as it also reacts with air and sometimes explodes.

47 A huge pile of snow consists of hardly any water

The ratio is about 1 cm (0.4 in) of rain equals 15 cm (6 in) of snow. That's because there's a lot of air between snowflakes, and snow takes up greater volume (more space) than the water it's made of.

Crump, crump

If you've ever been for a walk in the snow, you will have noticed that you leave deep footprints. That's because the snow under your feet is pressed down by the weight of your body, squeezing out some of the air between snowflakes. Your footprints are filled with compacted snow, or snow that has been pressed close together. Snowflakes are spiky shapes that don't fit together neatly as they fall, so a great deal of air is trapped in newly-fallen snow. Snow is a mix of ice crystals (snowflakes), liquid water (where some has melted), and air.

48 Snow is noisy

If you walk in fluffy snow, it's often silent. If the snow is cold or packed together it makes a sound when you tread on it. The warmer snow is, the more liquid water there is around the ice crystals. The water lets the ice crystals slide over each other. When there is little water, treading on them breaks the crystals, making a noise—usually a squeaky or creaky sound. In hard-packed snow, ice grains are bonded together. Treading on them breaks the bonds between crystals, making a different sound. This time it's crunchy!

Crunch!

49 Divers can get bubbly blood

And that's bad! A condition called "the bends"(or decompression sickness) can happen if a diver stays deep underwater for too long. This is caused by bubbles forming inside the body and not being able to escape.

Going down...

When you go underwater, the pressure of water on your body is greater than the pressure of air on it when you're on land. The deeper you go, the more water piles up above you and the greater the pressure becomes. A diver breathes in a mixture of nitrogen and oxygen from an air tank. The body needs the oxygen, but the nitrogen is a gas in the air we don't use. Under pressure, some of the gas dissolves in liquids in the body.

...coming up

As a diver rises again, the pressure drops. Rising slowly, there's time for the gases that have dissolved in the body to come out slowly. But if the diver comes up too quickly, the gas comes out of solution as bubbles inside the body. Bubbles of nitrogen form in the joints, making them hurt. They can form in blood, changing the blood pressure.

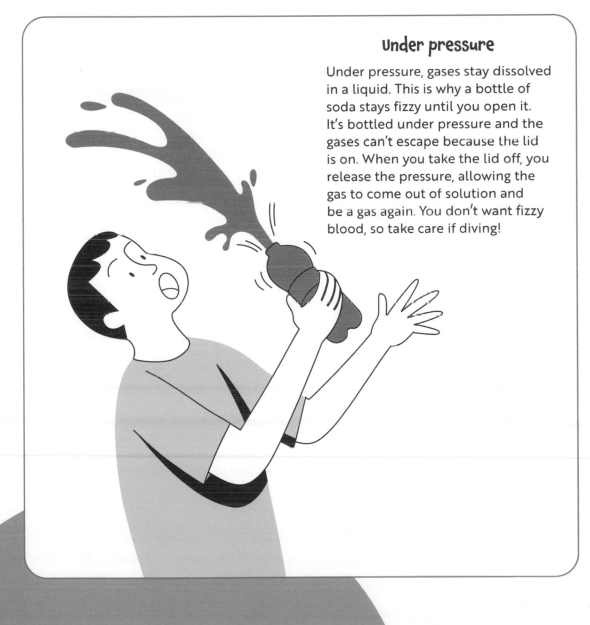

Under pressure

Under pressure, gases stay dissolved in a liquid. This is why a bottle of soda stays fizzy until you open it. It's bottled under pressure and the gases can't escape because the lid is on. When you take the lid off, you release the pressure, allowing the gas to come out of solution and be a gas again. You don't want fizzy blood, so take care if diving!

50 Much of your body is 13.8 billion years old

The first matter to appear after the Big Bang that started the Universe was the nuclei (middles) of hydrogen atoms. More than half the atoms in your body are hydrogen atoms.

You're only as old as you feel!

Simple start

The Universe started with a "Big Bang" when space–time and a lot of energy erupted from nowhere. Out of this super-hot mix, the first matter appeared. It was two types of tiny particle, called protons and neutrons. A proton has a positive electric charge. A neutron has no electrical charge. These particles appeared in the first second of the Universe's existence. Protons are hydrogen nuclei—the middles of hydrogen atoms.

Real matter

A hydrogen nucleus is a start, but it's still not actual hydrogen. To make a hydrogen atom, the proton needs to find an electron to pair up with. The electron orbits around the proton at a healthy distance, and the space between them makes the atom enormous compared to just its nucleus (but still very small compared to anything else).

Atoms formed from the mix of nuclei and electrons around 380,000 years after the Big Bang. That's not long in terms of the history of the Universe—but it's still as long as from the evolution of modern humans until today. For all that time, the Universe had no atoms!

We're matter, and we shall rule the Universe!

DID YOU KNOW?

Around 75 percent of all normal matter in the Universe is hydrogen. Almost all the rest of it is helium.

51 Every atom in your body was made in space

Your body is made of chemicals, and all the chemicals are made of atoms. Each atom is one of the chemical elements, and they were all made in space—either at the start of the Universe or in stars.

First things first

The first atomic nuclei to appear were hydrogen nuclei. In the first 20 minutes of the Universe, some hydrogen nuclei stuck together with neutrons and became helium, but that's pretty much all there was to start with. They became atoms a few hundred thousand years later when they gained electrons.

Making more

When some of the hydrogen atoms gathered together to make stars, they began to make more helium. The middle of a star is essentially a helium factory. It squashes hydrogen together to make helium. When the star gets old and starts to run out of hydrogen, it squashes helium together to make heavier atoms of different elements, all the way up to iron.

Supernova!

Some large stars come to an explosive end. They finally run out of atoms they can fuse. At that point, they collapse inward and explode dramatically. The explosion has so much energy, it fuses heavy atoms like iron into even heavier elements. And all the stuff that's been made in the star's life and death is blasted out into space. That's where all the atoms of Earth and other planets come from. And all the atoms in everything on Earth—including you.

52 Salt melts the ice on roads

Have you ever seen a truck spreading salt on icy roads in winter, or on roads that are expected to freeze overnight? The salt dissolves in water on the road's surface and lowers its freezing point. That means the temperature can drop below 0°C (32°F) and the road will be wet, but not icy. It won't freeze until it gets to about −6.5°C (20°F)

Squeezing between

When salt dissolves in water, the molecules of sodium chloride separate, becoming sodium ions and chloride ions. (An ion is an atom that has lost or gained electrons—so an atom with extra or missing "hands!") The ions are scattered around among the water molecules. They get in the way as the water tries to form a regular crystalline structure to make ice.

Frozen seas

Because the freezing point of salty water is lower than the freezing point of ordinary water, the sea rarely freezes, except in very cold places (like Antarctica). The ice that does form is less salty than the sea below it. The reluctant-to-melt salty water tends to sink.

Just add salt

You can also add salt to melt ice that has already formed. People sometimes sprinkle salt on their path to melt the ice and make it less slippery. It works because the salt dissolves in the very top layer of the ice: the sodium and chloride atoms sneaking in between the water. When that melts, the salt can move down a layer and melt the next bit of ice, and so on.

53 There are human-shaped molecules

Chemists have had fun making molecules of different shapes. By knowing how chemicals react together, they can predict the bonds the atoms will make in a chemical reaction and can control them to "sculpt" molecules to look as they want them to look.

Meet the NanoPutians

In 2003, a team of chemists at Rice University in Texas, USA, started making person-shaped molecules as part of an educational program to get kids interested in chemistry. They called the molecules "NanoPutians."

Invisible statues

NanoPutians are made of organic chemicals, so they're based mostly on bonds between carbon and hydrogen atoms. The body of a NanoPutian has two benzene rings (see pages 64–65), and the head is a pentagon (five-sided shape) made of carbon, hydrogen, and oxygen. Other bonds between carbon, hydrogen, and oxygen make the straight lines. The molecules are too small to see; we just have to take the scientists' word for it that there's a beaker of tiny NanoPutians on the bench.

A whole team

The first NanoPutian created was NanoKid, but you can't leave kids on their own, so the chemists soon created some adults to go with them. These are the NanoProfessionals. You can tell them apart by their hats:

NanoAthlete

NanoPilgrim

NanoGreenBeret

NanoJester

NanoMonarch

NanoTexan

NanoScholar

NanoBaker

NanoChef

Somewhere to live...

Obviously, these NanoPeople need somewhere to live. Luckily, chemists have also made molecules that look like buildings. These compounds are called Housane, Churchane, and Pagodane.

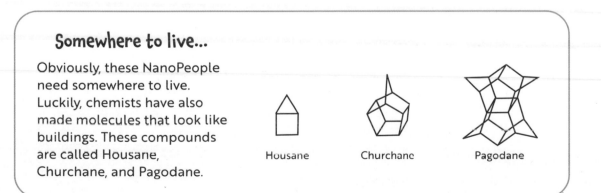
Housane   Churchane   Pagodane

54 We can tell what stars are made of from their light

When you look at the night sky, you see stars as bright twinkling spots of white light. But to astronomers and chemists, looking closely at the light from a star can show what it's made of. The spectrum of light, from red to violet, contains light of different colors. Chemicals absorb light of different colors. By looking at which colors reach us from a star, we can work out what's in the star.

Making light work

When a bright light shines through the gas, some light is absorbed by the chemicals in the gas. Scientists can see black lines in the spectrum where light of the missing color has been absorbed by cooler gases on the outside of the star. Stars are so hot that even chemicals that are solids on Earth are gases in a star.

A hot gas emits (gives out) light of the same color as it absorbs when it's cool. Chemists can identify a gas by the light it emits or absorbs.

Balls of gas

Stars are giant balls of gas, mostly hydrogen and helium. Helium absorbs yellow light and was first discovered when chemists in the 1860s found black lines in the spectrum of sunlight that didn't match any element known on Earth. By looking at the spectrum of a star and identifying the chemicals that produce the black lines, scientists work out what distant stars are made of.

55 Bad eggs float, but good eggs sink

If you've had some raw eggs hanging around for a bit, you can tell whether they are still good to eat by putting them in water. Bad eggs will float, because as they go bad, some of the liquid in the egg turns to gas and some of the gas escapes through the shell. That makes the egg light enough to float.

De-composing—it means taking apart

When we compose something, we put it together. When something decomposes, it comes apart. An egg (or anything else) that is going bad is decomposing. Chemical reactions are taking place in it that take apart the chemicals it's made of and make different chemicals. When something organic (once living) decomposes, a lot of gas is produced.

Gassy bodies

The living bodies of plants and animals are made of lots of different organic compounds. These compounds are made mostly of carbon and hydrogen, with other elements in smaller quantities. During decomposition, these compounds break down and the bits often form gases. Carbon and hydrogen make methane together. Carbon and oxygen make carbon dioxide. Hydrogen and oxygen make water. Gas molecules are tiny, and they can escape through the eggshell. As more of the matter of the egg escapes, the egg gets lighter.

Stinky eggs

Hydrogen and sulfur make a gas called hydrogen sulfide. This has the horrible smell we associate with bad eggs (and one of the smelly chemicals in farts!) Hydrogen sulfide molecules are too big to escape through the eggshell, but if you open a bad egg instead of testing it in water, you'll soon know it's bad!

56 The most expensive chemical on Earth is mostly carbon

Carbon is everywhere—in the air, in your body, in all the living things around you, and in most of Earth's rocks. But it comes in different forms. Pure carbon can be graphite, or it can be diamond, or it can be "buckminsterfullerene," or a few other things. The difference is in how the atoms are arranged. One of these arrangements, with an added nitrogen atom, makes a chemical called $N@C_{60}$ that costs $167 million a gram—or nearly $4.8 billion an ounce. The only thing more expensive is anti-matter!

Bucky balls

In graphite, the carbon atoms are arranged in layers that slide easily over each other. Diamond has a tetrahedral structure, with each carbon atom bonded to four others. Buckminsterfullerene has 60 carbon atoms arranged in a nearly spherical structure. It sounds pretty wild, but it occurs naturally in outer space! There are also tiny amounts of it in soot. These tiny spheres of carbon are often called "Bucky balls." They roll over each other, making Buckminsterfullerene a good lubricant.

Yes, I'd like this deposited in my bank account, please.

Trapped!

The most expensive chemical is an "endrohedral fullerene." It's a sphere of carbon atoms making a cage that traps a single nitrogen atom in the middle. Although the basic ingredients—carbon and nitrogen—are common, it's extremely difficult to make. Only 50 milligrams (one six-hundredth of an ounce) of $N@C_{60}$ can be made in a day, and it takes weeks to purify it.

57 Lobsters have blue blood

Your blood is red because it contains a compound called hemoglobin that uses iron to carry oxygen. Hemoglobin with oxygen makes human blood red. But lobsters—and spiders, octopus, and squids—use a different chemical to carry oxygen in their blood that makes a blue compound.

Blue bloods

Animals that have blue blood use a chemical called hemocyanin to carry oxygen around their bodies. In place of iron, this uses copper to bond with oxygen. Several compounds of copper are blue. You might have made copper sulfate crystals—these are bright blue. Or you might have seen an old copper roof that has gone greenish-blue over time, forming a compound called verdigris. Inside a lobster, the copper compound in the blood goes blue when it combines with oxygen.

Other bloods

Blue and red aren't the only options. Some types of worms and leeches have green blood. This uses a compound called chlorocruorin, which is light green until it combines with oxygen and then it goes properly green. Worms also have a bit of iron in there, and if there is a lot of oxygen in their blood, it attaches to the iron, too, and gives their blood a reddish tinge. Some types of marine (sea-dwelling) worms and shellfish even have violet blood. This contains hemerythrin. It's see-through without oxygen, but it goes pink-violet when it attaches to oxygen. Could you imagine what it would be like to have purple, green, or blue blood like these creatures?

58 Gold medals are made of silver

If you're hoping to win an Olympic gold medal so you have a good chunk of gold, think again. The gold medal is actually at least 92.5 percent silver, with a very thin coating of gold.

Cheapskates?

Gold is much more valuable than silver. Gold medals from the Tokyo Olympics in 2021 weighed 556 g (19.6 oz). The price of gold and silver changes all the time, but gold is generally worth nearly 100 times as much as silver. On a random day, silver cost $20 per oz (28 g), while gold cost $1,750 an oz. A solid silver medal would cost about $400 to make, but if it was entirely gold it would cost nearly $35,000!

Bendy medals

Gold is malleable. This means that it can be squashed and bent without breaking. It's a soft metal, and it can be easily hammered into a thin film. This is great for coating medals because it doesn't require much. Because it's soft and easily shaped, though, it's also easily bent and dented. A pure gold medal, while rather nice, would be easily damaged.

59 Only two metals don't look silvery

Copper and gold are the only two metals that don't look like silver. Silvery metals reflect light across the spectrum equally, but for very complicated reasons, gold and copper absorb more blue light and so look golden.

DID YOU KNOW?

Before 1912, Olympic gold medals really were made entirely of gold.

60 Adding salt to water makes it boil at a hotter temperature

People don't only add salt to the water when they boil rice, pasta, or potatoes to make their food taste salty. It also raises the temperature at which water boils; it means they can cook their food at a higher temperature and more quickly.

It's so attractive

Water molecules are loosely attracted to each other by hydrogen bonds. These form between the oxygen atom in one water molecule and a hydrogen atom in a nearby water molecule. For water to boil, these bonds have to be broken. The molecules move more as the water is heated until eventually they break free and escape into the air. But salt disrupts these bonds between the water molecules. It causes even more trouble, making stronger bonds with the water molecules itself. The sodium ions from the dissolved salt are attracted to the oxygen atoms, and the chloride ions are attracted to the hydrogen atoms.

Not enough energy

Bonds between the water molecules and the ions from the salt work to hold the water in place, not letting it escape into the air. That works for a while, but if the water gets too hot, it can still break free and turn into a gas. By then, the temperature of the water is hotter than its usual boiling point. The more salt you put in water, the more the boiling point rises. But too much will make your food taste nasty!

61 There are no atoms of the element organesson

Organesson is the element with the heaviest, largest atoms of all. It doesn't exist in nature and only five or six atoms have ever been created. Because it's radioactive, with a short half-life of just 0.9 milliseconds, none of the atoms still exists.

Here today, gone today

It's difficult to find out much about an element if there's only one or two atoms of it and they last less than a second. Chemists think organesson would probably be a gas at room temperature. From the number of electrons it has, it probably wouldn't be very reactive—it would be hard to make compounds using organesson and other elements.

It's possible that in a huge supernova, atoms could be crushed together to make organesson. It would still last less than a second before decaying, though. That means most of the time, there isn't any organesson anywhere in the Universe. But it could come and go.

62 You could have an element named after you

Many elements are named after famous scientists, such as einsteinium (after physicist Albert Einstein) and Curium (after chemist Marie Curie). When someone discovers a new element, they get to name it. It's not cool to name it after yourself, though.

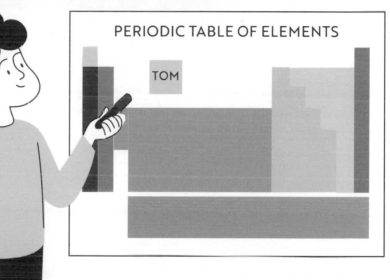

PERIODIC TABLE OF ELEMENTS

TOM

Your name here

So to get a new element named after you, you'll first have to become a famous scientist and, secondly, impress someone who finds a new element. But it's not cool to name an element after someone who is still alive. That means even if you do get an element named after you, you'll probably be dead and won't even know about it. Unfair!

63 Coffee keeps insects away...

...but only if you're a coffee plant. Coffee contains caffeine, the chemical that makes it a buzzy thing to drink. But while caffeine is a stimulant for humans, keeping us awake and wired, for insects that snack on coffee plants it's too much.

Chemical warfare

Many plants produced chemicals that help to protect them against attack by insects or larger animals that might want to eat them. Some are poisonous; others taste bitter or too spicy. Plants' chemical weapons don't always work against humans, though. We eat hot peppers precisely because they are spicy; we drink coffee because it stimulates us. But we're a lot bigger than an insect and have very different bodies.

Tea or coffee?

Coffee contains a stimulant called caffeine, and tea contains a stimulant called theine. But guess what? They're the same chemical! It's called caffeine if it's found in coffee and theine if it's found in tea. Coffee contains the most "caff-the-ine." Tea makes up for it by containing some other stimulants, but they're not as strong so coffee still wins in the keeping-you-awake stakes.

Even you...

You might not drink tea or coffee, which are natural sources of caffeine; however, if you drink cola, you will still get that jolt because caffeine is added to it. Caffeine occurs naturally in chocolate, too, so even if you only drink water, nibbling a chocolate bar gives you a caffeine hit. The darker the chocolate, the more caffeine it contains.

64 Bananas make fruit go bad

As fruit ripen, they produce a gas called ethylene. But ethylene is also a chemical that acts on fruit, making them carry out the changes we call ripening—getting softer and sweeter and often changing from green to yellow or red. Bananas produce a lot of ethylene, so putting them with other fruit can help to ripen unripe fruit. But ethylene also makes ripe fruit ripen even more, until it goes bad.

Chemical messages

Chemicals are used as "messengers" in all living things. In your body, chemicals produced in your stomach tell your brain when you've eaten enough and to stop feeling hungry. They tell your body something scary is around, and you should run away or hide. They tell your body to breathe faster if you're running so you can get more oxygen. Plants use chemicals in this way, too. Ethylene triggers chemical changes in fruit. As one bit of fruit ripens, it produces ethylene which can start other bits of nearby fruit ripening, too.

Take control of fruit

To ship fruit around the world, people control how and when it ripens. If it has to travel a long way, it's kept cold and stored in an atmosphere of nitrogen. Cold slows down all processes in living things, including ripening. Nitrogen is a gas the fruit and microbes on it can't use for anything. By keeping away oxygen and ethylene, the fruit stays unripe. If you buy unripe fruit, you can take control. Put it in a bowl on a sunny windowsill with a banana, and it will soon start to ripen.

65 Meteorites tell us what Earth is made of

Meteorites are rocks from space that fall to Earth. By studying them, scientists can work out what Earth was like when it first formed.

Dust and rocks

Earth, the other rocky planets in our solar system, and meteorites all formed together about 4.6 billion years ago. The planets formed as bits of dust and rock crashed together, growing into ever bigger lumps. But some lumps didn't grow to planet size and still hang around as large rocks in space. Every now and then, one crashes to Earth and we get the chance to check out the chemicals inside of it, which are basically the same materials that make up Earth—it's just that Earth has a lot more of them. Because Earth is so big, the heaviest bits have sunk to the middle where we can't reach them. Meteorites that fall to Earth help scientists figure out the composition (ingredients) of our home planet.

Moon rock

Some meteorites are actually bits of other planets (usually Mars) or the Moon. They're chunks that have been knocked off and thrown into space when asteroids have struck their home. Chemists can work out the composition of these rocks and tell what the outer surface of their source planet or moon is made of. We have Moon rock that was brought back by the Apollo missions, but meteorites from Mars that have fallen to Earth are the only source of Mars rock that scientists have been able to study.

66 Cats know some useful chemistry

If you have a cat, you might have seen it chewing and rolling in certain plants, such as catnip or silver vine. It seems this is good for both the cat and the plant—but not for bugs. The cat is using chemicals from the plant to look after itself.

"Keep-away" chemicals

Lots of plants produce chemicals that repel (keep away) bugs. The problem is, most of the chemical is inside the plant. When the leaves are damaged, the chemical is released into the air. These insect-scaring chemicals are volatile, which means they evaporate and turn to gas at a low temperature. When a cat chews or rolls in catnip, it breaks open many of the leaves. The chemical escapes into the air and is noticed by nearby bugs that might have been about to attack the plant—to eat it, to lay eggs on it, or perhaps take bits away.

Making more

Damage to the catnip leads the plant to make more of its "keep-away" chemical. It makes up to ten times more, which will protect it quite nicely from bugs.

And the cat?

By rolling around on a crushed catnip plant, a cat covers itself with the plant's bug-repellent. Among the bugs that the chemical scares away are mosquitoes, and it works better than mosquito repellents you can buy in a shop. The cat covers itself in chemicals that keep away annoying bugs—a great example of cats using chemistry! And a cat is a nice, furry way to keep away mosquitoes.

67 A small cube of gold can be turned into miles of wire

A chunk of gold weighing about 30 g (1 oz) can be spun into super-thin wire more than 100 km (60 mi) long. This is possible because gold is highly ductile, which means that it can be stretched out into thin pieces without breaking.

DID YOU KNOW?

Gold is so soft, it's possible to scratch it with a fingernail!

Easily shaped

The opposite of ductile is brittle: a brittle metal breaks when pulled out of shape. Because of the way the atoms of gold are arranged, gold can be pulled and hammered and deformed (forced out of shape) in other ways without ever breaking. This has made it useful and valuable throughout history. It can be bent into shape quite easily and hammered into such a thin sheet that it's almost see-through. As it's also pretty, sparkly, and very different from all the silvery metals—and it doesn't corrode or rust—gold has been used for thousands of years for making decorative and valuable objects, such as jewelry and crowns.

Soft metal

Gold is soft and can be shaped easily (see page 95). A lump of gold that weighs just 1 g (0.035 oz) can be beaten flat into a sheet covering 1 sq m (10 sq ft). Even without high-tech tools it can be reduced to a thickness of just 0.001 mm (0.00004 in). Because it can be made so thin and doesn't corrode, it's been used to cover parts of buildings— only a tiny amount is needed to give a beautiful golden sheen.

68 Diamonds and pencil lead are chemically the same

Pick up a pencil and draw. Do you know what's happening? Tiny particles of graphite are coming off your pencil tip and sticking on the page. Graphite is the chemical element carbon. Carbon can exist in different forms, including soot, graphite, and diamond. The "lead" (not really lead) in your pencil and soot from a fire are chemically the same as diamonds!

Tiny puzzle pieces

Everything in the Universe is made of atoms, the tiniest particles of matter. How atoms are arranged and combined give materials their properties. In a graphite pencil lead, the carbon atoms are arranged in flat sheets that slide over each other easily. As you draw, layers transfer to the paper.

In diamond, carbon atoms are arranged in a strong three-dimensional shape. This makes diamonds extremely hard.

Can you turn a pencil into diamond?

Not easily, but in theory it's possible. Sadly, it would be so difficult and expensive it wouldn't be worth it. It takes 150,000 times Earth's atmospheric (air) pressure to squash graphite enough to make it change into diamond.

69 Diamonds rain inside gas giant planets

It's hard to get enough pressure on Earth to make diamonds, but deep inside gas planets like Jupiter that kind of pressure is just part of everyday life. Lightning frees carbon from gases and it falls as soot. On the way down, it's squashed and squeezed into hard diamonds—and these fall as rain inside the planet. Diamonds might be the most common kind of rain in the solar system!

70 Water has a "skin"

You might have seen some insects that can stand on the surface of a pond. Mosquitoes can do it, and so can some beetles. They can do this because water has surface tension, which works like a kind of skin, meaning its top layer is tough to get through.

A tense surface

A drop of water on a hard surface like a tile or window looks curved. That's because surface tension holds it in a droplet shape. Surface tension is caused by the tendency of a liquid to pull together, to have the lowest surface area possible. As the shape with the least surface area of all is a sphere, water tends to make spherical drops. When a drop of water is on a solid surface, the bottom has to become flat, and it spreads out, but the rest can still be rounded.

Forces at work

In a glass of water, forces act between molecules of water equally in all directions. As these are equal, when an object is submerged it moves around in the water without the forces between molecules affecting it. At the surface, though, the forces between molecules are present only below and to the sides of each molecule. The molecules in the liquid are attracted more strongly to each other than to molecules in the gas above the surface. In water, hydrogen bonds between water molecules help to create surface tension.

If a light enough object lands on the surface, the bonds between water molecules stop the object falling through. If you're careful, you can even balance a steel needle on the surface of water.

71 Bleach can turn you to soap

Bleach is good at getting some things clean, but you should never use it to clean yourself. It can turn your body into soap, which might sound good for getting sparkly and spotless, but it really isn't!

Back to basics

Bleach is a basic solution, which means it has a chemical in it which is described as a "base," also called an alkali. It's the opposite of an acid, but it can be just as destructive as an acid. There are several different types of base that can be included in bleach, but they all work in the same way. The base attacks the fat molecules in your skin (or on something you're cleaning) and turns them to soap. The process is called "saponification," which means "turning to soap."

Making soaps

If you ever find yourself the sole survivor of a zombie apocalypse or other disaster, you can keep clean by making your own soap. Get some wood ash and soak it in water. That gives you a basic (alkaline) solution. Then add some liquid fat to it and stir a lot. It can be fat from an animal you have eaten, greasy wool from a sheep, milk, or even cooking oil.

72 Spicy foods can be spicy in two ways

The chemicals that make food spicy are the same in a lot of different foods. There are two different spicy chemicals: one makes things "hot spicy" and one makes things "cold spicy."

Hot and cold

The "hot spicy" chemical, capsaicin, is found in foods such as hot peppers. The "heat" of the peppers can even be measured using a special scale called the Scoville Scale. The "cold spicy" chemical is found in wasabi and mustard.

Spice at work

Chemicals like these affect special cells in your body called "receptors," which then trigger nerves to make you feel as though your mouth is burning. There are some receptors in other parts of your body, too. Never rub your eyes after cutting up hot peppers—they will feel burned.

73 Bleach doesn't really remove stains

People use bleach to kill germs and also to remove the stains from things that have got dirty. But bleach doesn't actually remove the smudges; it just hides them.

Fading away

Bleach breaks some of the bonds in the pigment molecules that give a stain color, and then the pigment can no longer reflect colored light. That means you can't see it any more. This is how hair bleach works, too. It might claim to strip the color from your hair, but it doesn't actually remove anything—it just breaks the pigment so it doesn't work as a pigment any more.

My bleached hair is completely stain free!

74 Eating silver turns you blue

It's never a good idea to eat anything that isn't actually sold as food, but some non-foods can have quite unexpected effects. Turning you blue—forever—is a pretty serious effect, but it's what can happen if you eat or drink things containing compounds of silver.

Don't try this at home!

The blue man

American Paul Karason made a concoction at home that he thought would be healthy, but it didn't do him any good at all. He made a solution that contained silver. He drank it and he smeared it on his skin in the hope of curing a skin condition he had. But the silver particles came out of solution and were carried around his blood stream, building up in his skin. Over a period of several years, he turned bluer and bluer—but he kept on using his solution because he claimed it improved his health, even if he was blue. He's not the only person to have turned blue from using silver-based medicines and creams.

Just like a photo

Old photographic plates worked because a solution of silver nitrate used on the plates turns black when exposed to light. The same reaction happens when skin containing silver salts is exposed to sunlight. It's important to remember that chemicals in your body react in just the same ways as if they were anywhere else. Chemicals don't care where they are!

DID YOU KNOW?

It's safe to eat gold because it doesn't react in your body. There are even gold-plated sweets!

75 Soda is fizzy because of your mouth, not just because of the soda

Soda and other fizzy drinks are fizzy to drink because of a process called "nucleation." This is the rapid release of the gas that makes the drink fizzy—carbon dioxide. Your mouth has a lot of "nucleation points," or sites that help the carbon dioxide escape.

It was okay in the bottle

Carbon dioxide is dissolved in soda, which is then put into a bottle or can. While it's in there, the carbon dioxide can't escape—there's nowhere for it to go. When you open the bottle or can, some gas escapes immediately, but not very much unless you shook it first. Not much escapes if you pour it into a glass, either, as a glass has very smooth sides.

Your fizzy mouth

The inside of your mouth is not smooth. Where there are dips and bumps in the surface, they work as "nucleation sites." Bubbles form at these points as the carbon dioxide comes out of solution—and that's what you experience as "fizz."

With extra gas

If you shake your soda, it fizzes more when you open it. Soda is bottled under pressure. While some carbon dioxide can come out of solution and make a small air space at the top of the bottle or can, most stays in solution. But if you shake it, even the escaped gas is mixed back in. It makes much bigger bubbles than the normal fizz-bubbles, though, and these escape quickly when you open the soda.

76 Mauve was discovered by a teenager

The first synthetic organic dye was created by a chemistry student in the 1850s. It was mauve, which had never been available before. It became hugely trendy!

Mauve against malaria

As an 18-year-old student, William Henry Perkin accidentally discovered mauve dye while trying to find a cure for malaria. Quinine, the treatment for malaria, was expensive, as it came only from a type of tree regional to South America. Perkin and his professor tried to make quinine in the lab, and Perkin continued working on the problem in his home laboratory. He made a right mess, which turned out to be mauve dye. Ever on the ball, Perkin developed his dye and sold it, becoming a millionaire before he was 21. Suddenly, everyone was wearing mauve

Sneaky molecule

Perkin's new chemical was called "mauveine." As often happens in chemistry, people discover a substance, or how to make it, before they understand the chemistry of it. The molecule of mauveine wasn't fully understood until 1994. It was then given the much trickier name of 3-amino-2,9-dimethyl-5-phenyl-7 (p-tolylamino) phenazine acetate. Most people stick to mauveine.

DID YOU KNOW?

Roman emperors liked to wear purple robes, which were made using a dye taken from sea snails. It took A LOT of snails, so it was expensive. The snails probably weren't so keen on this fashion!

77 You contain enough carbon to make thousands of pencils

The "lead" in a pencil isn't lead at all—it's graphite, which is a form of carbon. Your body is made mostly of chemicals that are combinations (compounds) of carbon, hydrogen, nitrogen, oxygen, and some other elements.

The write material

There's so much carbon in a human body that if we could take it all out, we could make the lead for 10,000 pencils from each adult. On the whole, you're probably more useful as a person than as 10,000 pencils, so we won't try it.

You're organic

Chemists call compounds that are made mostly of carbon and hydrogen "organic" compounds. They are essential to all living things, and living things are called "organisms"—so organic compounds make organisms. (But it's got nothing to do with organic foods or organic farming.) Many organic compounds have very large molecules containing hundreds or thousands of atoms. They make up every part of you, from blood to skin and from hair to muscle and even bone.

If you disintegrate...

If we could take a person apart and return them to the chemical elements that make up all the different substances in their body, we'd be left with a lot of gas, a lot of potential pencil leads, and a tiny pile of solid crystals. Besides the carbon, you're mostly made of gases: hydrogen, nitrogen, and oxygen are all gases at room temperature. Taken apart, most of you would just drift off into the air.

Glossary

Acid: A chemical compound that is soluble in water and tastes sour.

Alchemist: An early type of chemist, interested in changing other material to gold and searching for a potion that would give people everlasting life.

Atmosphere: A layer of gases kept around a planet, star, or other object by its gravity.

Atom: The smallest possible particle of a chemical element.

Bacteria: Tiny organisms with just a single cell (single "bacterium"). Some bacteria cause disease, but many are helpful to us.

Big Bang: The start of the Universe with the instant appearance of a tiny, hot, dense point from which all matter and energy has expanded.

Bond: A link between atoms.

Carbon dioxide: A waste gas produced by living things, made up of one carbon atom bonded to two oxygen atoms.

Chemical reaction: Two or more chemicals reacting together, making and breaking the chemicals' bonds.

Compound: A substance made of more than one of the chemical elements, held together by chemical bonds.

Concoction: A mixture made of several ingredients.

Condense: Change from a gas to a liquid.

Core: The very middle of something.

Corrode: Become destroyed or damaged through chemical action. Rusting iron is an example of corrosion.

Decompression: Reducing the pressure something is under.

Density: The weight of a substance compared to the amount of space it fills.

DNA: Deoxyribonucleic acid, the chemical that makes up chromosomes in a living thing and which carries a "code" in its structure that acts as instructions for making the organism.

Ductile: Capable of being drawn out into a long wire.

Electric current: The flow of electrons that produces electricity.

Electron: Tiny particle with a negative electrical charge. They are the smallest parts of atoms; the flow of electrons produces electricity.

Element: One of the 118 chemicals that cannot be broken down into simpler chemicals.

Energy: The power to perform work.

Evaporate: To turn from liquid into gas.

Flammable: Able to burn.

Freeze: To turn from liquid into a solid through getting cold.

Friction: A force that slows moving objects.

Gas: A substance that is like air and has no fixed shape.

Gravitational: Produced by gravity.

Gravitational field: The space in which gravity operates around an object. Gravity is a force that works between objects with mass, drawing them together.

Gravity: A force that works between objects with mass, drawing them together.

Helium: A gas, the second lightest chemical element.

Hydrogen: A gas, the lightest chemical element.

Hydrogen bond: A weak bond between hydrogen atoms.

Impurities: Bits of something that shouldn't be in a substance, preventing it from being pure.

Latex: A bendy, stretchy substance like rubber.

Liquid: A substance that flows to fill the shape of a container or over a surface, like water.

Mantle: The layer of the Earth just below the crust (where we live). It's made of hot, very slow moving, semi-molten rock.

Mass: A measure of how much matter there is in an object.

Mesopotamia: An ancient land and culture in the area that is now Iraq.

Molecule: The smallest possible unit of a substance that still behaves like that substance. A molecule is made up of two or more atoms.

Neutron: A tiny particle with no electric charge in the middle of an atom.

Nucleus: The middle of an atom, made of protons and neutrons.

Orbit: A fixed path taken by one object in space around another because of the effect of gravity.

Organic compound: One of a huge range of chemical compounds containing carbon that is found in living things.

Organism: A living thing.

Oxygen: A gas that is essential for life.

Periodic Table: The chart of 118 chemical elements arranged in order of their atomic number, which relates to how many protons are in the nucleus of the elements' atoms.

Pigment: A substance used to dye or add color to something

Planet: A world orbiting a star that has enough mass and gravity to pull itself into a sphere, and clear space in its orbit of other large objects.

Pressure: The force of one object or substance pressing on another

Proton: A tiny positively charged particle in the middle of an atom.

Radio antenna: A piece of metal, often shaped as a rod or dish, which is used to send out or pick up radio waves.

Reactive: Readily takes part in chemical reactions, which involve two or more chemicals reacting together, making and breaking chemicals bonds.

Silicate rock: Rock based on the element silicon.

Solar System: The eight planets (including Earth) and their moons, and other objects such as asteroids, which orbit around the Sun.

Spectrum: Full range of visible light, from red to violet, like a rainbow.

Spontaneously: Suddenly, without preparation or warning.

Spore: A cell that can grow into a new organism, as a seed or egg can do. Bacteria and fungi reproduce from spores.

Stimulant: A chemical that makes someone feel more awake and lively.

Submerged: Completely under the surface of a liquid.

Supernova: A massive explosion that comes at the end of a large star's life.

Telescope: A tool that collects light or other radiation from space and uses it to create an image.

Temperature: The measure of heat.

Trillion: A million million (1,000,000,000,000).

Tropical: In the warm region near the equator.

Vibrate: Tiny shaking movements.

Volume: Space occupied by a substance or object, or within a container.

Index